This book is dedicated to the Integration of Western Medicine and Food-Based Healing.

Supreme Science Qigong Center was founded in 1999 and became Press on Qi Productions in the year 2008. We've organized and created hundreds of seminars with many respected veteran Qigong Practitioners from all over the world. As time progresses we are aware that results matter most. That is why we combine Food Based Healing with Qigong exercise. Together, dietary practice combined with Qigong forms a complete self-healing program.

Special Thanks to Our Teachers

Over the course of direct personal study for more than 15 yrs, many teachers have revealed great amounts of food healing wisdom to me in case-by-case fashion. This knowledge can belong to no man... as it is God's plan for our healing.

We have personally interviewed countless people who overcame so-called irreversible cancer, heart disease, diabetes, autism, tumors etc. Many of these people attended our Qigong Healing seminars and got well using Dietary Truth. I have acquired this food-healing wisdom from many sources including several well known Qigong Masters, Naturopathic Doctors and a decade of intense research. Many thousands of people worldwide have used this same Food-Healing wisdom to reverse the most serious diseases of our time. It is amazing the *degree of healing* that is possible with little more than the foods from the grocery store! Many diseases respond to specific vegetables, fruits and common household herbs. I believe it is the simplicity of the teaching that makes it work. My grandparents, uncles/aunts, mother/father—they all do it. So can you.

*This information is not meant to treat, prevent, or cure any disease and is not endorsed by the FDA.
*Please share this information with your health care provider before making any changes to your diet.
*Please know that we have taken pain staking measures to verify the accuracy of these writings to the very best of our ability.
*Photocopying and Plagiarizing is prohibited. Written permission can be obtained to reference for true educational purposes.

The Superfoods within this Book

Most of what you need can be found in the organic produce section of your favorite grocery store. Some superfoods like Maca & Goji Berries are of lower quality at most stores. My recommendations are FREE OF COMMERCIAL BIAS. Usually I choose the most **cost effective** products available, but quality must never be sacrificed when seeking to create a strong physical body. There are a few items in that I frequently recommend of superior quality that are not found at most health food or grocery stores.

In the spirit of convenience, I have asked my friend Richard Pearl of Simply Natural Health Food Store in Sunrise, Florida to create a website where all the great products are in 1 place at the lowest prices. Food-Healing.com is maintained by the loving people who work with him. Simply Natural has served South Florida for over 14 years and people drive from far away just to buy from his knowledgeable staff. Richard also runs an organic restaurant serving delicious food and many special foods inside this book. We are blessed that readers will be able to obtain all the herbs and superfoods in one central location.

Simply Natural
Organic Cafe
8267 Sunset Strip
Sunrise, FL 33322

www.Food-Healing.com

JOIN US ON THE
Radio!
Pearls of Health Radio Show
With Hosts: Richard Pearl & Sharooz Taheri
WMCU AM 1080 SATURDAY 10-11 AM
Listen live at www.1080wmcu.com

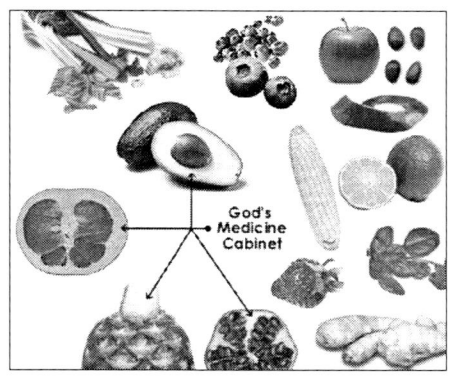

Smoothie Formulas

Based on a Whole Food Approach to Healing

"And God said, "Behold, I have given you every herb bearing seed, which is upon the face of all the Earth, and every tree, in which is a tree yielding seed; to you it shall be for meat."
- Genesis Verse 1:29

Hello my friends,

Welcome to the world of 3 horsepower blending! This powerful blender will break out the phytochemicals hidden in the stems, skin, seeds, rinds, fibers and flesh of fruits and vegetables down to the micron level! These wondrous phytochemicals help your body heal and regenerate in amazing ways. Once you start blending with a 3 horsepower blender on a regular basis you are going to love the way it makes you feel. In addition, blending has quick preparation time and clean up—so this way of living will be easy for you to sustain.

Do your best to include all appropriate skins, stems and seeds from washed fruits and veggies in your smoothies. The avocado seed is extremely high in soluble fiber and phytochemicals, which is excellent for helping to clean out your arteries, lower cholesterol, and it has *the energy of an entire tree!* Do your best to buy organic ingredients when possible and when unavailable to use veggie wash.

Those with type 1 or 2 Diabetes are asked to use only vegetables in their smoothies. No fruit whatsoever, except for the lime. We have chosen specific veggies with "Insulin-like Substances" that can naturally bring down your blood sugar. There are case histories of thousands of people to who <u>naturally</u> manage Diabetes using dietary principles alone. This is a simple diet: Veggies, Beans, & Seafood. The Diabetic MUST give up all starches & fruits, which spike the blood sugar. This is only if the Diabetic desires a natural food-based solution. The bitter melon recipes in this book were made especially for you.

Food-based Healing is a very powerful artform and there is a LOT to learn. We created a 125 page manual that covers every detail you could ever want to know about which foods for specific health problems. This book also covers all the foods you need to avoid and crucial knowledge about how to heal faster. It's called: "Conquering ANY Disease—The Ultimate High-Phytochemical Food Healing System". This manual has the most complete information on how to heal the body using food of any book ever written. We encourage you to learn exactly why these recipes were chosen... and how to prepare cooked meals. There is a lot more to know that just smoothies, but they are the KEY to healing. The particles of Cellulose fiber, which contain the phytochemicals, get broken down on the micron level. This is the secret as to why people have reversed nearly every disease using smoothies. When people asked for specific recipes that TASTED GOOD and followed the principles of this Food Healing System—this manual was slowly born. Now it is the 7th edition and it's the ultimate collection of our most loved "Smoothie Formulas" for their taste & healing power. Your transformation will be larger than life.

All Formulas have the same blender operation. Place ingredients in blender and hold down the "pulse" button for 15 seconds. Then let go and press the up arrow until it revs up to "Speed 10". It will cycle up to speed 10 and stop automatically after 50 seconds. Blend for a minimum of 2 cycles for about 2 minutes. Often we like to blend for 3 cycles to REALLY break everything down, but that requires two ice cubes to keep the contents from getting overly hot. Ice is a welcome ingredient if your like me and do not like smoothies warm. It also allows you to blend for more cycles without heat damaging the nutrients. Please Note: *If you are blending for 1 person you may want to cut recipes in half to avoid wasting food.* Fresh smoothies do not store well for more than 4 hours. Do not blend your smoothie at night before bed to drink in the morning! If you are pressed for time try putting all the ingredients in plastic bags and then simply drop them into the blender in the morning.

Peace & Love,
Jeff Primack

P.S. - If you are fortunate to have access to fresh Turmeric Roots we highly suggest using them. Turmeric complements recipes calling for ginger with even more phytochemicals.

Smoothie Formulas
Based on the High-Phytochemical Food Healing System

"Prove your servants, I beg you, ten days; and let them give us vegetables to eat, and water to drink. Then let our faces be looked on before you, and then the face of the youths who eat of the king's dainties; So he listened to them in this matter, and proved them ten days. At the end of ten days their faces appeared fairer, and they were fatter in flesh, than all the youths who ate of the king's dainties. So the steward took away their dainties & wine that they should drink and gave them vegetables." Daniel 1:12-16

Part 1: Smoothies for Specific Health Issues

Page 6:	Autism: Ultimate Chelating Smoothie
Page 6:	Autism: Mellow Chelating Smoothie
Page 7:	Brain Function: Mind Power Smoothie
Page 7:	Brain Function: Coffee Replace Smoothie
Page 8:	Cancer Fighting: The Cancer Crusher 1
Page 8:	Cancer Fighting: The Cancer Crusher 2
Page 9:	Cancer Fighting: The Cancer Crusher 3
Page 9:	Cancer Fighting: The Cancer Crusher 4
Page 10:	Cancer Fighting: Super Citrus Smoothie
Page 10:	Cancer Fighting: The Alkalizer Smoothie
Page 11:	Constipation: Bad Qi go out Smoothie
Page 11:	Constipation: Qi Clearing Smoothie
Page 12:	Cough: Heavenly Throat Smoothie
Page 12:	Depression: Free Your Mind Smoothie
Page 13:	Diabetes: Bitter Mellon Sunshine Smoothie
Page 13:	Diabetes: Bitter Mellon Crimson Smoothie
Page 14:	Diabetes: Swiss Chard Cucumber Smoothie
Page 14:	Diabetes: Chef's Choice Cucumber Smoothie
Page 15:	Eye & Vision: Bright Eyes Smoothie
Page 15:	Eye & Vision: See Clearly Smoothie
Page 16:	Heart Disease: Artery Scrubber Smoothie
Page 16:	Heart Disease: Mexican Heart Healer Smoothie
Page 17:	Heart Disease: Lower Pressure Now Smoothie
Page 17:	Heart Disease: Awaken Circulation Smoothie
Page 18:	Kidney Stones: Watermelon Dissolver Smoothie
Page 18:	Lung Disease: Breathe Deep Smoothie
Page 19:	Male Sexuality: Strong Like Bull Smoothie
Page 19:	Female Sexuality: Jing Power Smoothie
Page 20:	Osteoporosis: Bones of Steel Smoothie
Page 20:	Osteoporosis: Silica Blast Smoothie
Page 21:	Pain/Arthritis: Anti-Inflammation Smoothie
Page 21:	Stomach Issues: Yummy Tummy Smoothie

Part 2: Smoothies for Maintaining Excellent Health

Page 23:	Jeff's Most Recommended Smoothie
Page 23:	Jeff's Classic Vegetable Smoothie
Page 24:	Anne's Infamous Spicy V8
Page 24:	Phytochemical Blast Smoothie
Page 25:	Mighty Green Smoothie 1
Page 25:	Mighty Green Smoothie 2
Page 26:	Broccoli Stem Bliss 1
Page 26:	Broccoli Stem Bliss 2
Page 27:	Anti-Oxidant Bliss Smoothie
Page 27:	Strawberry Surprise Smoothie
Page 28:	BEET the Disease Smoothie
Page 28:	Power Beet Smoothie
Page 29:	Pineapple Enzyme Smoothie
Page 29:	Amazing Light Green Smoothie
Page 30:	Beta Carotene Smoothie
Page 30:	Happy Heart Smoothie
Page 31:	Advanced Pomelo Take Away Evil
Page 31:	Advanced Pomegranate Formula

Part 3: Smoothies for Healthy Kids (fruit based)

Page 33:	Blueberry Surprise Smoothie
Page 33:	Pineapple Sunshine Smoothie
Page 34:	Purple Sky Smoothie
Page 34:	Tropical Sunset Smoothie
Page 35:	Berry Bliss Smoothie
Page 35:	Kids Can Do It Too Smoothie
Page 36:	Papayaraz Perfection Smoothie
Page 36:	Easy Tummy Smoothie
Page 37:	Autism Cilantro Blast for Kids V1
Page 37:	Autism Cilantro Blast for Kids V2
Page 38:	Autism Cilantro Blast for Kids V3
Page 38:	Autism Cilantro Blast for Kids V4

Part 4: Healing Ice Cream ™, Hi-Vibe Deserts & Nut Milks

Page 40:	The FAT in Healing Ice Cream ™
Page 41:	Healing Ice Cream #1: Key Lime Goji Bliss
Page 42:	Healing Ice Cream #2: Chocolate Empowerment
Page 43:	Healing Ice Cream #3: Butter Pecan Mango
Page 44:	Healing Ice Cream #4: Virgin Coconut Paradise
Page 45:	Healing Ice Cream #5: Acai Berry Purple Haze
Page 46:	Healing Ice Cream #6: Maca Machoman Maple
Page 47:	Healing Ice Cream #7: Black Sesame Jing Blastoff
Page 48:	Chocolate Hazelnut Mousse
Page 48:	Chocolate Almond Mint Brew
Page 49:	Maca Cacao Manuka Honey Truffles
Page 50:	Creamy Sunshine Pudding
Page 50:	Goji Berry Milk—Jeff's Favorite
Page 51:	Almond Milk
Page 51:	Hazelnut Milk
Page 51:	Oat Milk
Page 52:	Pumpkin Seed Milk
Page 52:	Brown Rice Milk
Page 52:	Anne's Special Golden Milk
Page 53:	Jeff's Creamy Superfood Smoothie
Page 53:	High Vibes Chocolate Milk
Page 54:	Almond Strawberry Delight
Page 54:	Almond Apple Veggie Delight

Part 5: Soups, Salads & Bitter Mellon Dishes for Diabetics

Page 56:	Anne's Bitter Mellon Dahl
Page 57:	Anne's Bitter Mellon Curry
Page 58:	Swiss Chard Salad w/ Live Ginger Dressing
Page 59:	Watercress Salad w/ Walnut Avocado Herb Dressing
Page 60:	Darla's Chakra Salad with affirmations
Page 61:	Autumn Stew
Page 62:	Creamy Cucumber Avocado Soup
Page 63:	Creamy Asparagus Soup
Page 64:	Dietrie's Very Veggie Soup
Page 65:	Lively Tomato Basil Soup
Page 66:	Curried Cauliflower Soup

Part 1
Smoothies for Specific Health Issues

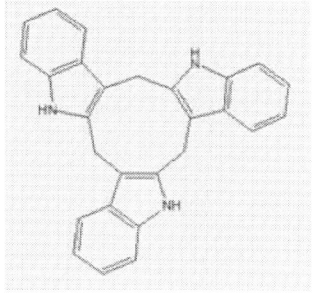

Food is Medicine
Not created by human
beings prone to mistakes...

For: Autism & Heavy Metals   "Ultimate Chelating Smoothie"

1 ½ c. distilled water
7 nodes of cilantro with stems
1 avocado with seed
1 organic cucumber with skin
1 fuji apple w/skin & seeds
1" slice ginger root
3 fresh basil tops
½ lime w/white pith

For: Autism & Heavy Metals   "Mellow Chelating Smoothie"

1 ½ c. distilled water
5 nodes of cilantro with stems
 (Increase as Tolerable)
8 organic strawberries
1 organic cucumber with skin
1 fuji apple w/skin & seeds
1" slice ginger root
½ lime w/ pith & seeds

For: Brain Function "Mind Power Smoothie"

1½ c. distilled water
2 ears fresh corn cut from cob
¼ c. raw pumpkin seeds
2 oz. organic goji berries
½ lemon w/ pith & seeds
½ inch fresh ginger root
3 nodes fresh cilantro

For: Brain Function "Coffee Replacement Smoothie"

2 c. distilled water
2 ears fresh corn cut from cob
2 carrots
1 fuji apple w/skin & seeds
1 small yellow beet
1 fist parsley with stems
2 tsp. bee pollen
(last 20 seconds of blending)
2 tsp. hempnut or flax seed
1" slice ginger root
2 fresh basil tops w/stem
½ lemon w/ pith & seeds

For: Cancer Fighting   "Cancer Crusher V1"

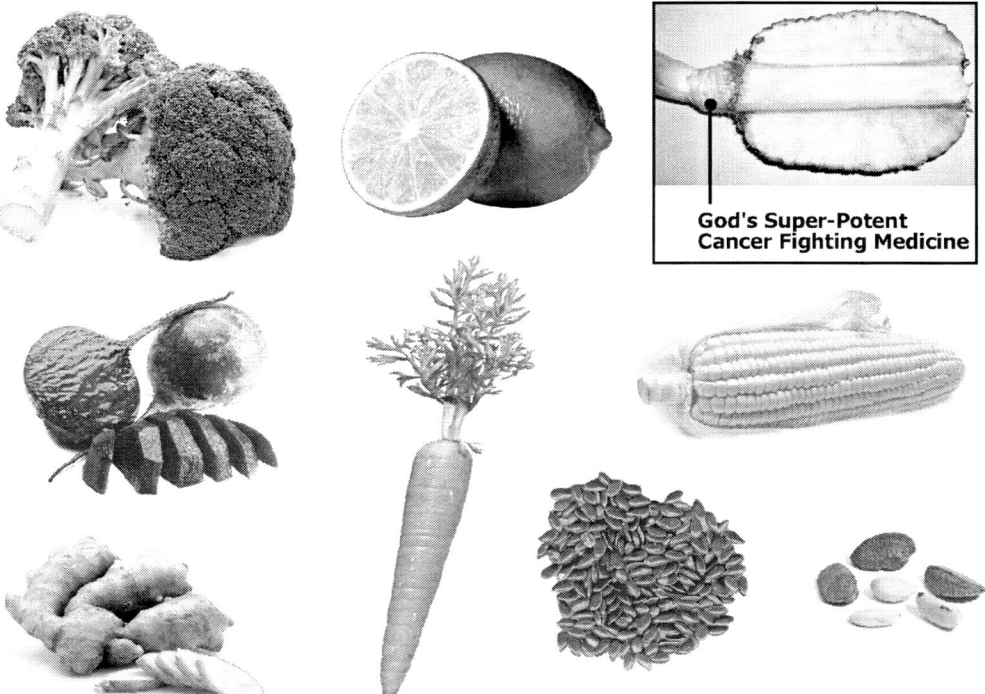

God's Super-Potent Cancer Fighting Medicine

3 c. distilled water
1 broccoli stem (not top floweret)
1 Pineapple Stem By Itself
(see CAD manual)
1 ear fresh corn cut from cob
1 carrot
½ small red beet
5 brazil nuts
½ lime, w/ pith & seeds
(last 20 seconds blending)
2 tsp. hemp or flax seed
1" slice ginger root

This is an advanced Smoothie.
Add organic strawberries if needed, but better without for people with cancer.

For: Cancer Fighting   "Cancer Crusher V2"

2-3 c. distilled water
1 Pineapple Stem By Itself
(see CAD manual)
1/4 red cabbage with white base
1 ear fresh corn cut from cob
1 carrot
½ small red beet
5 brazil nuts
½ lime w/ pith & seeds
2 tsp. bee pollen
2 tsp. hemp or flax seed
1" slice ginger root

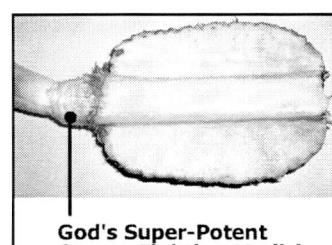

God's Super-Potent Cancer Fighting Medicine

This is an advanced Smoothie.
Add organic strawberries if needed, but better without for people with cancer.

8

For: Cancer Fighting   "Cancer Crusher V3"   *Easier

1 1/2 c. distilled water
5 fresh Brussel sprouts
1 fuji apple sliced with skin and seeds
1 vine ripe tomato
1 carrot
1 ear of corn cut from cob
½ lime w/ pith & seeds
1" slice ginger root

For: Cancer Fighting   "Cancer Crusher V4"   *Easier

1 1/2 c. distilled water
1/4 head purple cabbage
1 small red beet
½ lime w/ pith & seeds
1 fuji apple w/skin & seeds
1 carrot
1" slice ginger root
3 fresh basil tops w/stem

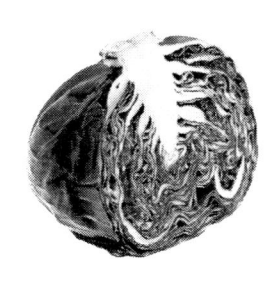
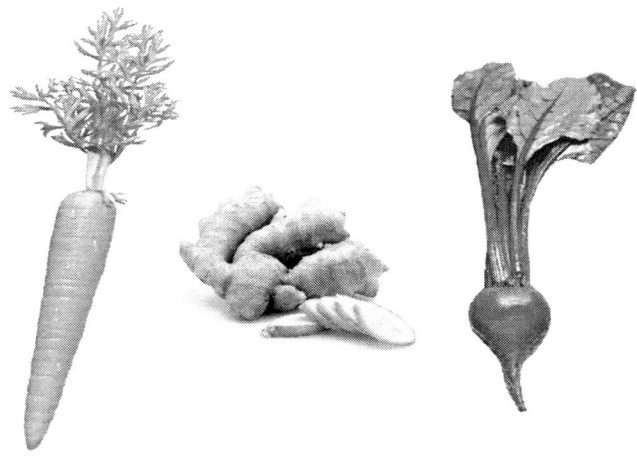

For: Cancer Fighting   "Super Citrus Smoothie"

1 ½ c. distilled water
1 grapefruit, leave white fuzz & seeds
1 orange w/ pith & seeds
½ lemon w/ pith & seeds
1 Fuji apple sliced with skin & seeds
½ ear of corn cut from cob
1" slice ginger root

Peel Away Outermost Skin
Leave Maximum White Part

For: Cancer Fighting   "The Alkalizer Smoothie"

1 ½ c. distilled water
3 stalks of organic celery
½ organic cucumber
½ lime w/ pith & seeds
1 Fuji apple sliced with skin & seeds
3 leaves of Swiss Chard
1 node of cilantro

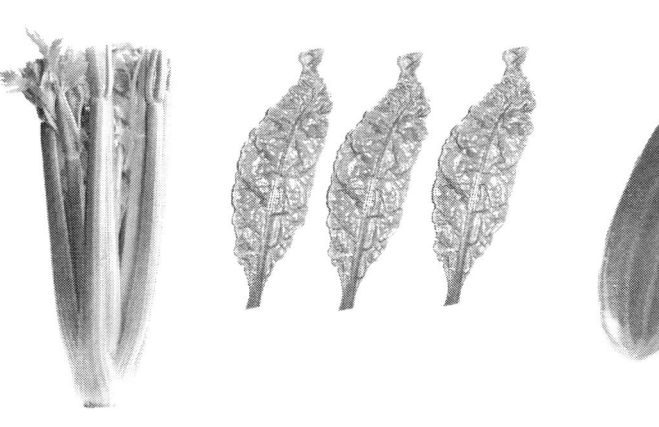

For: Constipation "Bad Qi Go Out Smoothie"

3 c. distilled water
5 sun dried prunes
(soaked for five hours)
½ Red Beet
¼ c. raw hazelnuts
1 fuji apple w/seeds
1 handful raw spinach
1 corn cut from cob
½ lime w/ pith & seeds
¼ tsp. cinnamon powder
4 T. Black Sesame seed

*Note: For chronic constipation you also need to repopulate the large intestine with friendly bacteria. We recommend taking "Good Belly", a probiotic and vitamin supplement that is wheat, dairy and soy free. Drink water first thing each morning. Immediately afterwards take 1 Good Belly day for ninety days. Good Belly may be taken on an empty stomach up to 3 times a day.

The best herbs for chronic constipation are called "Super 2" by Harmony Formulas.
Each night before bed take 1 or more Super 2's as needed. See CAD manual for more details.

For: Constipation "Qi Clearing Fruit & Fiber Smoothie"

2c. distilled water
1 fuji apple with skin & seeds
8 oz. pint Blueberries
¼ c. soaked hazelnuts
3 dried or fresh organic figs

For: Cough "Heavenly Throat Smoothie"

2 c. distilled water
3 radishes w/tops
1 tsp. licorice powder
1 corn cut from cob
1 fuji apple w/skin & seeds
½ lime w/ pith & seeds
1 T. agave nectar

For: Depression "Free Your Mind Smoothie"

2 c. distilled water
2 sprigs fresh rosemary leaves
1 corn cut from cob
5-10 organic strawberries
1 fuji apple w/skin & seeds
½ lime w/ pith & seeds
1 T. maca powder

Maca Root Powder

For: Diabetes   "Bitter Melon Sunshine Smoothie"

2 c. distilled water
½ bitter melon w/seeds (5 inches)
1 yellow beet, peeled
1 small carrot
3 Swiss chard leaves w/stems
½ lemon w/ pith & seeds
½ large organic cucumber
1" fresh ginger root
Pinch of Green Stevia (not white)

Insulin Like Substance

For: Diabetes   "Bitter Melon Crimson Smoothie"

2 c. distilled water
½ bitter melon w/seeds
½ small red beet
3 Swiss chard leaves w/ stems
½ large organic cucumber
½ lime w/ pith & seeds
1" fresh ginger root

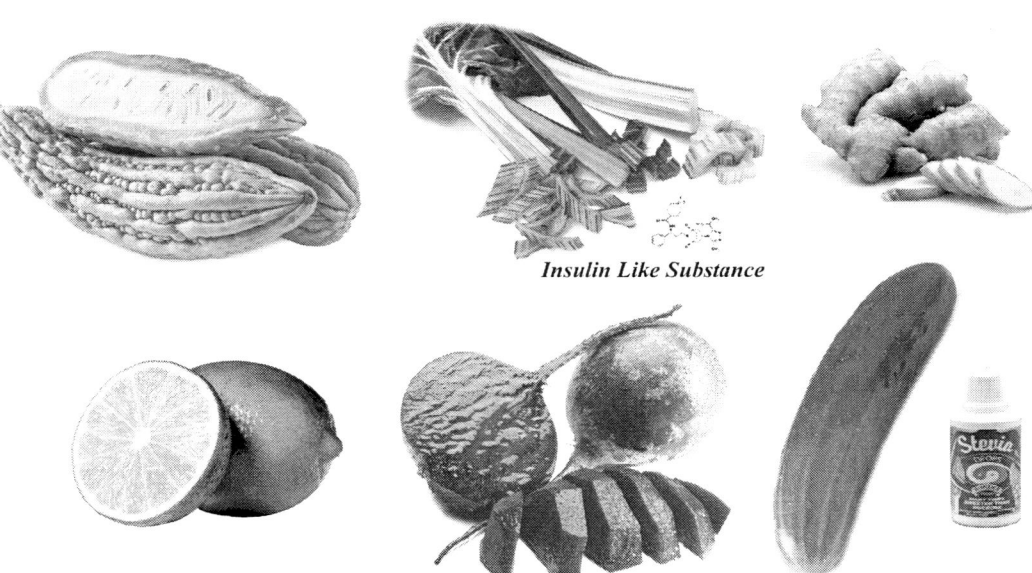

Insulin Like Substance

For: Diabetes "Swiss Chard Cucumber Smoothie"

2½ c. distilled water
4 large leaves Swiss chard
½ yellow beet
1 organic cucumber w/skin
½ lime w/ pith & seeds
1 ear corn cut from cob
1" slice ginger root
3 tsp. hemp or flax seed
Pinch of Green Stevia

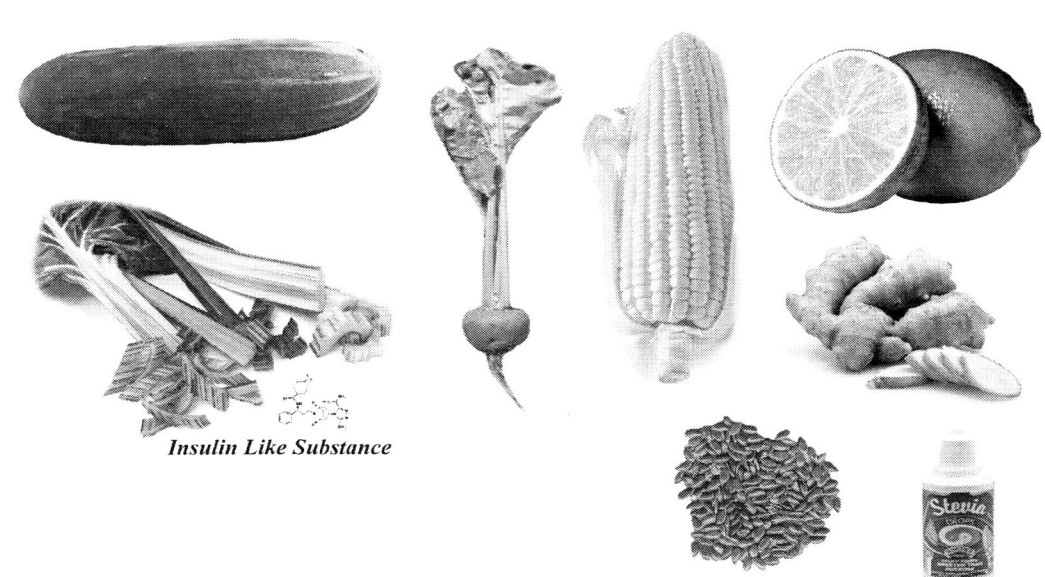

Insulin Like Substance

For: Diabetes "Chef's Choice Cucumber Smoothie"

1½ c. distilled water
2 organic cucumbers with skin
½ lime w/ pith & seeds
5 fresh mint leaves + stem
2 tsp. agave nectar
6 ice cubes
1 tsp. Turmeric Powder
1 pinch of cinnamon powder
2 organic strawberries for garnish

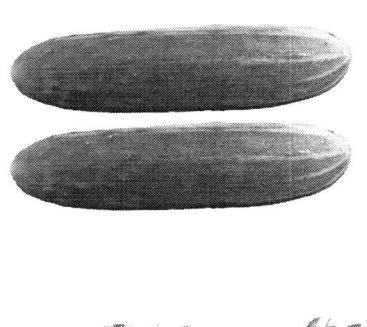

For: Eyes & Vision "Bright Eyes Smoothie"

2½ c. distilled water
1 handful of spinach
1 ear corn cut from cob
4 oz. blueberries
2 oz organic goji berries
½ fuji apple w/seeds
1 orange bell pepper
½ small red beet
½ lime w/pith

For: Eyes & Vision "See Clearly Smoothie"

2 c. distilled water
1 orange bell pepper w/ seeds
2 ears fresh corn cut from cob
1 carrot
1 Fuji apple w/seeds
2 oz. organic goji berries
½ lemon w/pith and seeds
2 nodes fresh cilantro

For: Heart Disease "Artery Scrubber Smoothie"

2 c. distilled water
1 dried woodear mushroom
 (soak overnight and blend)
½ avocado, with whole seed
½ red bell pepper with seeds
5 organic strawberries
1 ear of corn cut from cob
3 okra
2 fresh basil tops w/stem
½ small red beet
1" slice ginger root
½ lime w/pith

For: Heart Disease "Mexican Heart Healer Smoothie"

2 c. distilled water
1 dried black fungus mushroom
 (soak overnight and blend)
1 avocado with seed
Fruit pods of 1/2 pomegranate
1 large carrot
½ organic cucumber
3 okra
½ lime w/ pith & seeds
½ small red beet
1 fist cilantro

For: Heart Disease   "Lower Pressure Now Smoothie"

1½ c. distilled water
1 large organic cucumber
5 stalks celery
1 handful organic strawberries
3 large fresh mint leaves
½ lime with pith

For: Heart Disease   "Awaken Circulation Smoothie"

1½ c. distilled water
3 inches of ginger root
1 handful organic strawberries
3 large fresh mint leaves
½ lime with pith
½ cucumber
1 carrot
½ small red beet

For: Kidney Stones "Watermelon Dissolver Smoothie"

½ c. distilled water
4 c. cut watermelon w/ white flesh
(remove outer green skin w/ vegetable peeler)
6 ice cubes
Blend one cycle only

For: Lung Diseases "Breathe Deep Smoothie"

2 c. distilled water
2 white corn cut from the cob
5 fresh mint leaves + stem
1-2 spring onions
2 carrots
1" slice ginger root
8 oz Organic Strawberries
1 small handful of Parsley
2 T. organic goji berries

For: Male Sexuality "Strong Like Bull Smoothie"

3 c. distilled water
4 T. raw pumpkin seeds
½ pomegranate fruit (no white part)
4 oz fresh blueberries
2 vine ripe tomatoes
1 carrot
½ fuji apple
½ small red beet
1 lime w/ pith & seeds
1 T. maca root powder
1 tsp. turmeric powder

Maca Root Powder

For: Female Sexuality "Jing Power Smoothie"

2 c. distilled water
4 T. raw pumpkin seeds
1 T. maca root powder
1 handful organic strawberries
2 corn cut off cob
2 oz. goji berries
1 pinch of cinnamon
¼ c. black sesame seeds

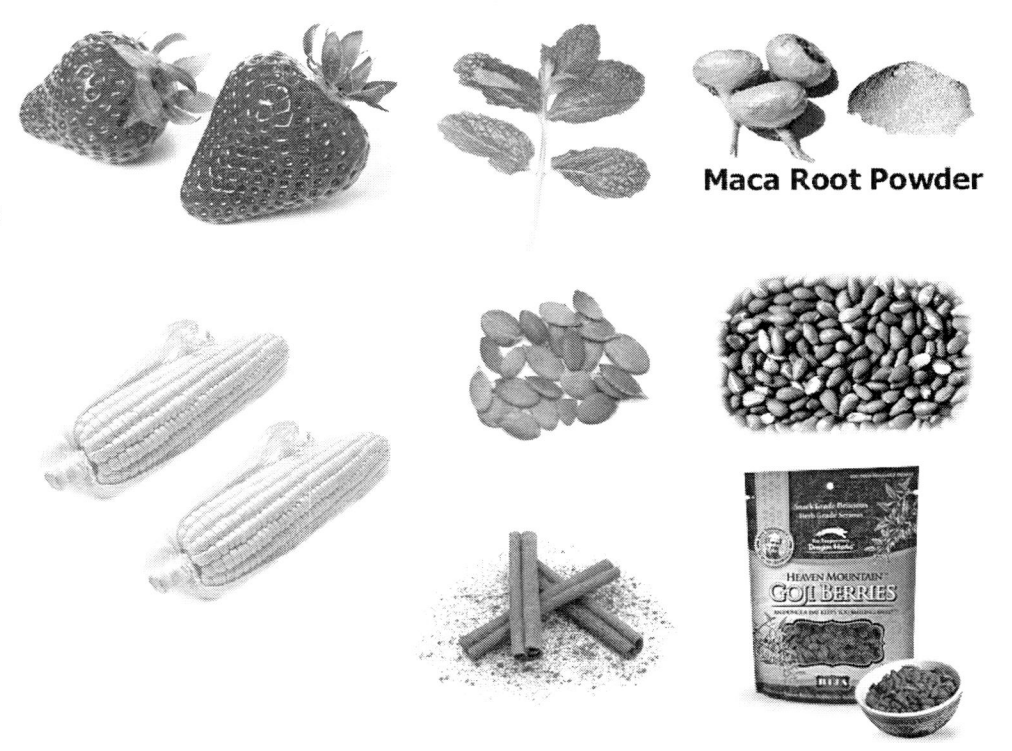

Maca Root Powder

For: Osteoporosis "Bones of Steel Smoothie"

2 c. distilled water
2 ripe plums with kernel
(use nut cracker to remove from pit)
3 sun dried figs
½ fuji apple with seeds
2 carrots
1" slice ginger root
2 organic cucumbers
½ lime w/ pith & seeds
2 T. organic goji berries

For: Osteoporosis "Silica Blast Smoothie"

2½ c. distilled water
2 ripe plums with kernel
(use nut cracker to remove from pit)
2 organic cucumbers
¼ c. pumpkin seeds
1 ear of corn cut from cob
¼ tsp. ground cinnamon
1" slice ginger root

For: Pain/Arthritis "Anti-Inflammation Smoothie"

2c. distilled water
30 cherries, remove pits
½ organic cucumber
1 small papaya w/out seeds
1 pineapple stem
1" pineapple slice
1 oz. Goji berries
2 nodes fresh cilantro
1" slice fresh ginger
1 tsp. turmeric powder

God's Super-Potent Cancer Fighting Medicine

For: Stomach Issues "Yummy Tummy Smoothie"

2 c. distilled water
¼ green cabbage w/ core
1 large apple w/ skin & seeds
1 whole clove (yes only ONE)
1" fresh ginger root
3 large mint leaves

Part 2
Smoothies for Excellent Health

For: Excellent Health   "Jeff's Most Recommended Smoothie"

2½ c. distilled water
8oz. organic strawberries
1 ear corn cut from cob
1 avocado with seed
1 fresh basil top w/stem
2 fresh mint tops w/stem
3 nodes fresh cilantro
1 inch of Rosemary
1 oz. Goji Berries
½ small red beet
½ organic cucumber
½ fuji apple w/seeds
½ lime w/pith

For: Excellent Health   "Jeff's Classic Vegetable Smoothie"

2 c. distilled water
½ yellow beet
1 vine ripe tomato
½ organic cucumber
1 corn cut from cob
1 avocado with seed
½ fuji apple w/seeds
½ lime w/pith
2 fresh basil tops
1" slice ginger root
2 tsp. hemp or flax seed

For: Excellent Health   "Anne's Infamous Spicy V8 Smoothie"

2c. distilled water
3 vine ripe tomatoes
2 stalks celery
2 carrots
¼ small red beet
1 organic cucumber
½ red bell pepper
1 fist parsley & cilantro
1 lime w/ pith & seeds
1" fresh ginger root
2 fresh basil tops
1 pinch sea salt
5 drops cayenne juice
  (more or less to taste)

For: Excellent Health   "Phytochemical Blast Smoothie"

2 c. distilled water
8oz. organic strawberries
4oz. fresh blueberries
4oz. fresh raspberries
2 fresh basil tops w/stem
1½" sprig rosemary leaves
3 fresh mint tops w/stem
1" slice ginger root
½ lime w/ pith & seeds

For: Excellent Health   "Mighty Green Smoothie V1"

3 c. distilled water
½ c. packed spinach leaves
½ organic cucumber
2 Swiss chard leaves
½ lime w/ pith & seeds
1 avocado with seed
1 fist parsley
1 small yellow beet
1 carrot
2 fresh basil tops/stems
1" slice ginger root
1 T. agave nectar (optional)

For: Excellent Health   "Mighty Green Smoothie V2"

3 c. distilled water
½ c. packed spinach leaves
½ organic cucumber
2 Swiss chard leaves
½ lime w/pith
1 ear of corn cut from cob
1 vine ripe tomato
1 small red beet
1 carrot
2 fresh basil tops w/stem
1" slice ginger root
1 T. agave nectar (optional)

For: Excellent Health   "Broccoli Stem Bliss V1"

2 c. distilled water
1 broccoli stem (not top floweret)
3 Swiss chard leaves w/stems
½ small red beet
1 fresh corn cut from cob
½ fuji apple with seeds
½ lime w/ pith & seeds
½ avocado with whole seed
½" slice fresh ginger root

For: Excellent Health   "Broccoli Stem Bliss V2"

2 c. distilled water
1 broccoli stem (not top floweret)
3 large leaves Swiss chard
½ fuji apple with seeds
½ lime w/ pith & seeds
½ avocado with whole seed
½" slice fresh ginger root
½ organic cucumber
1 pint organic strawberries

For: Excellent Health   "Anti-Oxidant Bliss Smoothie"

1½ c. distilled water
2 c. Muscadine grapes
½ pint fresh blueberries
½ fuji apple w/seeds
2 T. goji berries
½ lime w/ pith & seeds
½" slice fresh ginger root

For: Excellent Health   "Strawberry Surprise Smoothie"

2 c. distilled water
1 carrot
½ small red beet
½ fresh corn cut from cob
½ fuji apple with seeds
1 pint organic strawberries
½ orange w/ pith & seeds
½ lime w/ pith & seeds
½ avocado w/seed
1 fist parsley with stems
½" slice fresh ginger root

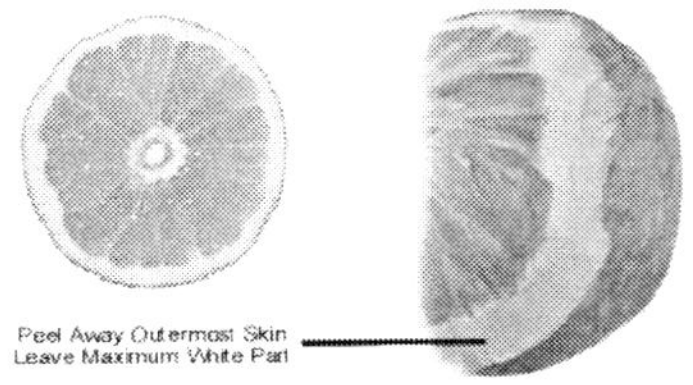

For: Excellent Health   "BEET the Disease Smoothie"

2c. distilled water
1 red beet, peeled
2 carrots
1 fuji apple
1 organic cucumber
1 fresh basil top
1 fist fresh parsley
½ lime w/ pith & seeds
1" fresh ginger root

For: Excellent Health   "Power Beet Smoothie"

1½c. distilled water
1 small red beet
½ pint blueberries
½ pint blackberries
1 pint organic strawberries
2 fresh basil tops w/stem
1" fresh ginger root
½ lime w/ pith & seeds

For: Excellent Health   "Pineapple Enzyme Smoothie"

1½ c. distilled water
¼ pineapple w/core & white stem
1 ear of corn cut from cob
1 fist parsley with stems
1 carrot
½ fuji apple w/core

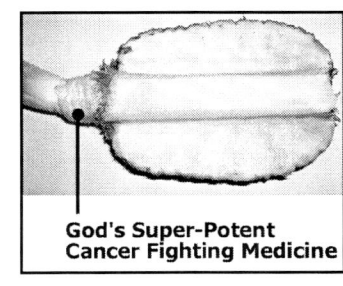

God's Super-Potent Cancer Fighting Medicine

For: Excellent Health   "Amazing Light Green Smoothie"

1 c. distilled water
1 Granny Smith apple
2 stalks celery
1 small carrot
1 fist parsley & cilantro
1 T. hemp or flax seed
1 T. bee pollen
½ lime w/ pith
1" fresh ginger root

For: Excellent Health   "Beta Carotene Smoothie"

2 c. distilled water
3 carrots
1 fuji apple, quartered
1 orange w/ pith & seeds
½ lemon w/ pith & seeds
½ peeled red beet
2 T. organic goji berries
1" fresh ginger root

For: Excellent Health   "Happy Heart Smoothie"

1 ½ c. distilled water
1 small red beet
1 ear corn cut from cob
1 valencia orange w/pith
½ lemon w/pith and seeds
2 oz. organic Goji berries
1" slice fresh ginger root
2 mint tops w/ stem
1 sprig fresh rosemary

For: Excellent Health   "Advanced Pomelo Take Away Evil"

2 c. distilled water
½ Pomelo w/pith, outer peel removed
All the fruit from both halves
1" fresh ginger root
2 fresh mint tops w/stem

God's Super Potent Cancer-Fighting Medicine

For: Excellent Health   "Advanced Pomegranate Formula"

2 c. distilled water
½ Pomegranate with white part & peel removed
All the fruit from both halves
1" fresh ginger root
2 fresh mint tops w/stem

White Stuff (Phytochemicals)

Fruit Pods & Seed

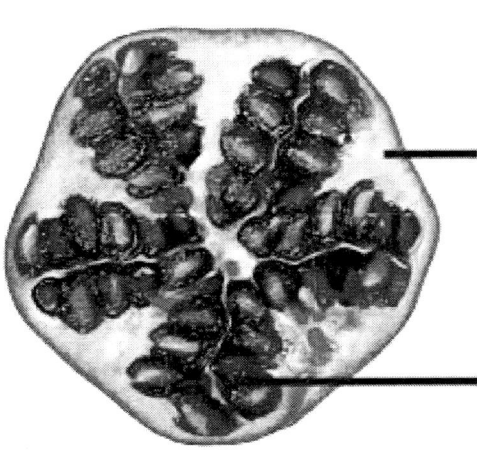

Part 3
Smoothies for Healthy Kids
~Fruit Based Formulas~

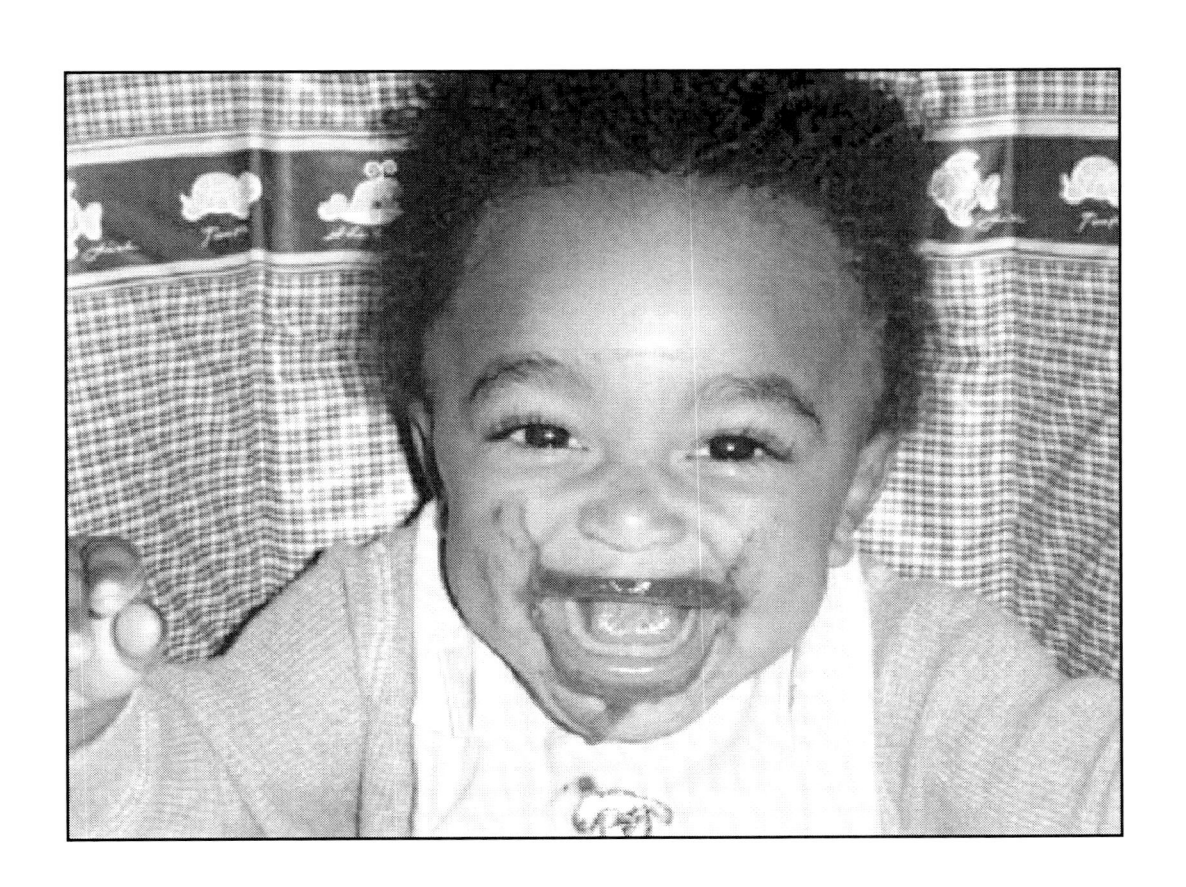

For: Healthy Kids   "Blueberry Surprise Smoothie"

1 cup distilled water
1 cup blueberries
1/2 lime w/white fuzz
1/2 orange w/white fuzz
2 Mint leave tops w/stem
2 ice cubes of distilled water

Peel Away Outermost Skin
Leave Maximum White Part

For: Healthy Kids   "Pineapple Sunshine Smoothie"

All you need to do is follow the pictures. Yank out all the green leaves until your left with the white stub on top. This is where the magic of pineapple is. Just be sure not to cut so close to the base where the stem is very "woody" as getting splinters of wood in your teeth is not cool. Add 4 oz of distilled water and 6 pineapple wedges. Blend on high 2 cycles with ice. Yum!

33

For: Healthy Kids "Purple Sky Smoothie"

1 cup distilled water
1 cup blueberries
1/2 orange w/white fuzz
4 oz. organic strawberries
1/2 sliced ginger
2 ice cubes of distilled water

Peel Away Outermost Skin
Leave Maximum White Part

For: Healthy Kids "Tropical Sunset Smoothie"

1 cup distilled water
4 oz organic strawberries w/tops
1 ripe peeled kiwi
1 orange w/white fuzz & seeds
3 mint leave tops w/stem
1/2 lime leave white fuzz & seeds
1/2 sliced ginger

Peel Away Outermost Skin
Leave Maximum White Part

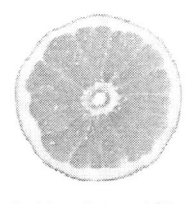

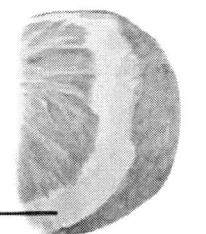

For: Healthy Kids "Berry Bliss Smoothie"

1 cup distilled water
1 cup organic strawberries w/tops
1/2 fuji apple with core
1/2 lemon w/white fuzz
1/2 inch sliced ginger
2 icecubes of distilled water

For: Healthy Kids "Kids Can Do It Too Smoothie"

1 cup distilled water
1/2 ruby red grapefruit w/ fuzz & seeds
1 fuji apple
4oz organic strawberries w/tops
1/2 orange w/white fuzz & seeds
3 mint leave tops w/stem
1/2 inch sliced ginger
2 icecubes of distilled water

Peel Away Outermost Skin
Leave Maximum White Part

For: Healthy Kids   "Papayaraz Perfection Smoothie"

2 c. distilled water
1 large papaya, peeled no seeds
½ pint fresh organic raspberries
½ ripe avocado <u>without seed</u>
1 ripe kiwi, peeled
½ inch ginger root
3 fresh mint leaves
¼ lime w/ pith

For: Healthy Kids   "Easy Tummy Smoothie"

1 ½ c. distilled water
1 organic cucumber, w/ skin
1 stalk celery
½ Fuji apple w/ skin and seeds
2 ripe Kiwi, peeled
½ lemon w/ pith and seeds
½ inch fresh ginger root
5 fresh mint leaves
1 Tbls. extra virgin coconut oil
1 tsp. agave nectar (optional)

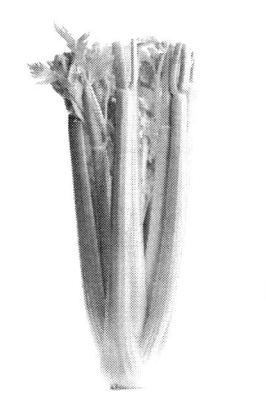

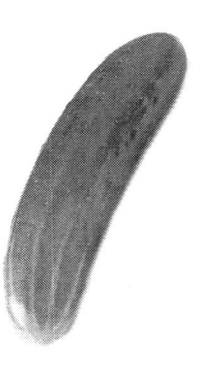

For: Healthy Kids   "Autism Cilantro Blast for Kids V1"

1,2,3,4,5,6 or up to 7 nodes of cilantro
8 oz of organic strawberries
4 oz distilled water.

My experience working with Autistic kids is that most are finicky eaters. Start out the smoothie experience on the right foot by limiting the amount of Cilantro and adding more gradually. We know that Autistic kids need more cilantro to get out the heavy metals, but it can be too strong a taste if overdone. In fact, cilantro over done tastes pretty bad. Start with 1-2 nodes (connection points where many stems connect). After the 1st one... if accepted and gulped down by the child, which is usually the case, you can add 1 more node each day until you reach the point that even you won't drink it. My favorite fruit to begin the journey is Strawberry.

For: Healthy Kids   "Autism Cilantro Blast for Kids V2"

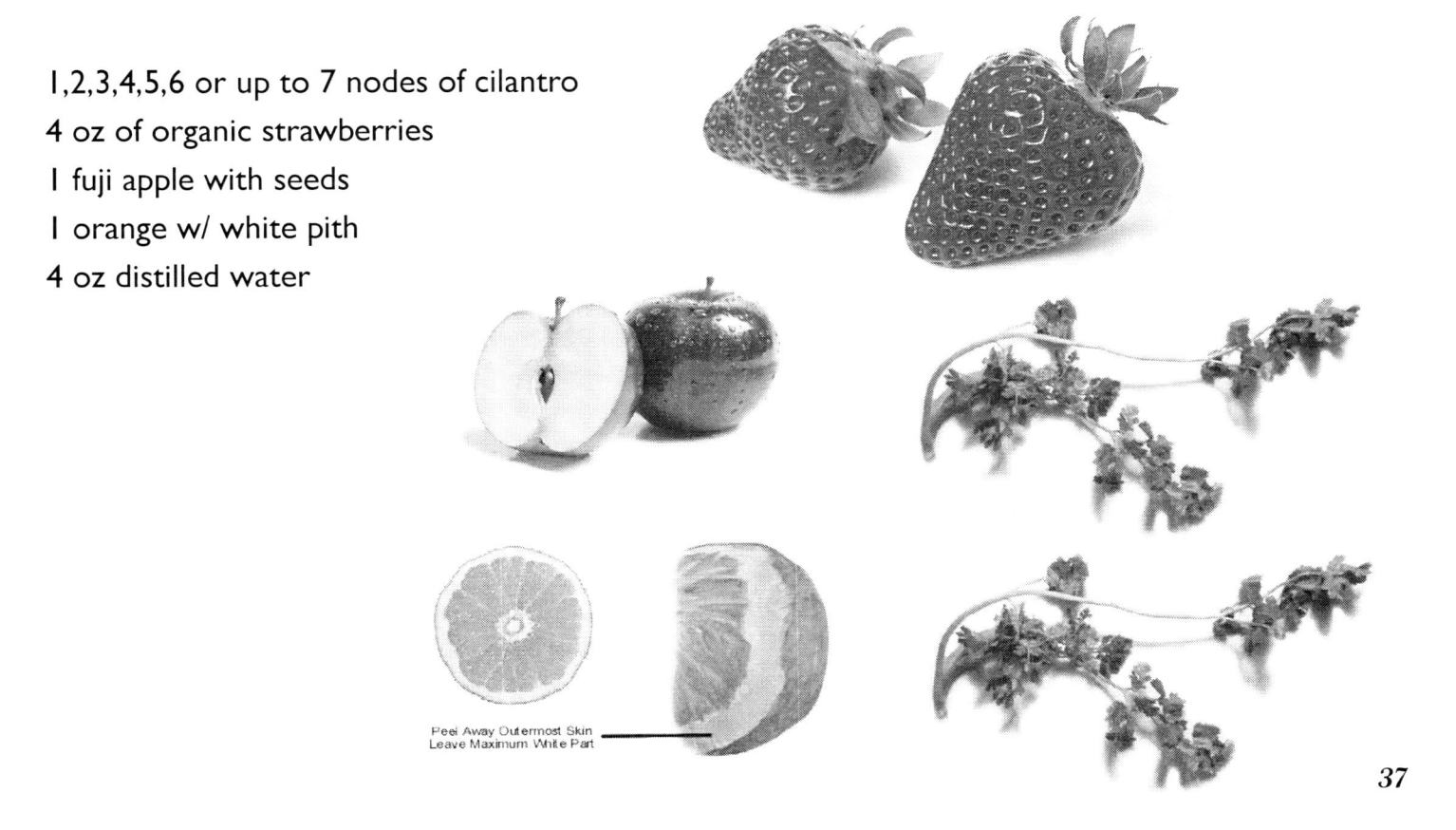

1,2,3,4,5,6 or up to 7 nodes of cilantro
4 oz of organic strawberries
1 fuji apple with seeds
1 orange w/ white pith
4 oz distilled water

Peel Away Outermost Skin
Leave Maximum White Part

For: Healthy Kids "Autism Cilantro Blast for Kids V3"

1,2,3,4,5,6 or up to 7 nodes of cilantro
4 oz of organic strawberries
1 corn cut from cob
½ organic cucumber
½ fuji apple w/seeds
8 oz distilled water

For: Healthy Kids "Autism Cilantro Blast for Kids V4"

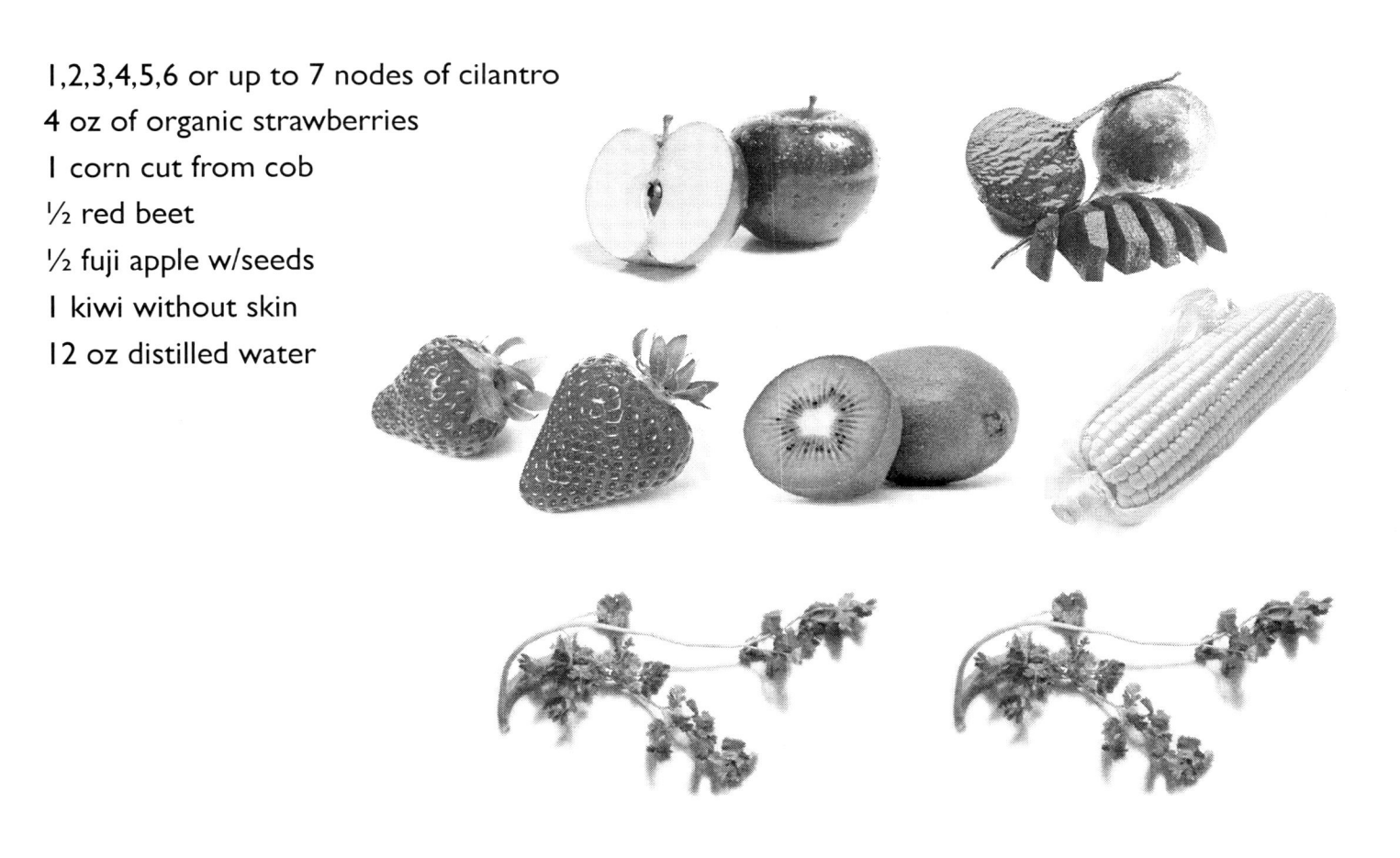

1,2,3,4,5,6 or up to 7 nodes of cilantro
4 oz of organic strawberries
1 corn cut from cob
½ red beet
½ fuji apple w/seeds
1 kiwi without skin
12 oz distilled water

Part 4: Healing Ice Cream ™ Special Deserts & Nut Milks

Desert Disclaimer:

Many people begin the Smoothie Program and High-Phytochemical Diet for different reasons. If you are fighting ANY serious disease you are asked NOT to embark on the desert section. While these recipes are rich in phytochemicals... they have more sugar. For the person fighting cancer, diabetes or ANY serious disease these types of foods would be very counter productive. If you are working on overcoming a disease it is best to avoid the deserts entirely.

For those who are reasonably healthy... these deserts using raw living foods taste BETTER than deserts you can get at a restaurant. My favorite are the RAW High-Phytochemical Ice Creams! Even though these foods taste AMAZING because they are living and full of energy... we still advise eating these foods *in moderation*. After all—this is a Food-Healing System. Balance is key. These High-Phytochemical Deserts are also a great to help people transition into a healthy lifestyle.

The FAT in Healing Ice Cream ™

The most deficient component of most people's diet is HEALTHY fats and oils. Our brain requires high levels of healthy fats to function and so does our metabolism. Fat is the "oil in the lamp" that gives rise to bright light. So it is great news that these recipes are high in beneficial fats. Omega 3's are the number one most deficient oil in the modern day diet and they are higher in Walnuts than any other vegetarian food. The fats in Coconut heal the gastrointestinal track and encourage the generation of inner heat, metabolism and weight loss. Macadamias, Pecans, Almonds and especially Black Sesame contain fats that INCREASE METABOLISM and are highly beneficial for health. The nuts used in these Ice Creams are also rich in minerals, vitamins & phytochemcials. We felt it important to acknowledge the wonderful healing properties behind the FAT in these Healing Ice Creams ™. People do not get heart disease from high fat diets... they get it from the wrong kinds of fats. These nuts are the right kind of fats for a healthy, long burning oil lamp. Now be the light and shine on the world!

Healing Ice Cream™ #1
Key Lime Goji Bliss

- Jeff's Favorite Ice Cream of ALL-TIME

About this Recipe:

The SSQ High-Phytochemical Food Healing System is based on the notion that phytochemicals are the real food for the immune system. In our opinion, Goji Berries are the most powerful food on Earth for their high protein, mineral and glyco-nutrient profile. No other food on earth has more glyco-nutrients than Goji Berries and these help your body's cells to communicate. Goji Berries have 50 times more beta-carotene than carrots and can dramatically help the body fight against asthma and eye diseases.

The benefits of taking Goji Berries daily cannot be over-hyped as long as they are not juiced and sit in a bottle for weeks and months waiting to be consumed. The best way to take Goji Berries is to blend them in a 3 Horsepower Blender. You can read in the Conquering ANY Disease yellow book all about Goji Berries and their huge importance for radiant health and fighting many diseases.

Key Lime Goji Bliss Ice Cream is a delicious way to enjoy the health benefits of Goji Berry.

1¼ cup Raw Macadamia nuts rinsed, chopped and soaked overnight in 1½ c. warm water

4oz. Heaven Mountain Goji Berries (half bag)

2/3 cup Raw Agave Nectar

½ Organic Lime - Outer Green Zest Peel

½ Organic Lime - Juice & Pulp (white pith makes it a little bitter, but has more phytochemicals)

Instructions:

Blend in 3 Horsepower Blender the soaked macadamias, 1½ c. distilled water, 4oz. Goji Berries, 2/3 cup agave, lime zest, pulp and juice on highest speed for two 50 second cycles.
Pour the mix into a 1.5 quart ice cream maker and freeze.
Makes 1 quart of Key Lime Goji Bliss Healing Ice Cream ™.

Healing Ice Cream ™ #2
Chocolate Empowerment

- If you're a Chocolate Lover… this is Heaven!

About this Recipe:

The SSQ High-Phytochemical Food Healing System is BIG on Raw Chocolate! A study of 8000 male Harvard graduates showed that chocoholics lived longer than abstainers. Their longevity may be explained by the high "polyphenol" levels in chocolate. Polyphenols reduce the oxidation of low-density lipoproteins and thereby protect against heart disease. Chocolate gives energy to the heart so it can function better. It is also a great mood enhancer and has been observed to contribute to longevity. You can read about the many benefits of chocolate in the Conquering ANY Disease yellow book.

There are many ways to eat chocolate. Anne makes a special Maca-Cacao truffle with a whole Cacao bean inside that is sooooo good! Another is Chocolate Empowerment ice cream. Truly a RAW chocolate wonder!

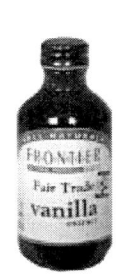

1/4 cup Raw Organic Premium Quality Cacao Nibs
2/3 cup Raw Organic Premium Quality Cacao Powder
2 Tablespoons Raw Organic Premium Quality Cacao Butter melted in 1 ½ Cups Warm Water
2 cups Blanched Raw Organic Almonds soaked overnight and rinsed
1 cup Raw Agave Nectar
½ teaspoon organic vanilla powder -or- 1 tsp. vanilla extract
10 drops peppermint oil (optional)

Instructions:

Blend almonds, cocoa butter with the water on 1 high speed cycle for 50 seconds. Add remaining ingredients <u>except cacao nibs</u> and blend on high speed one more 50 second cycle. Pour into 1.5 quart ice cream and freeze as directed. Stir in nibs 'after' ice cream is done. *Makes 1 quart of Chocolate Empowerment Healing Ice Cream ™.*

Healing Ice Cream ™ #3
Butter Pecan Mango

- Tastes <u>Better</u> than Regular Ice Cream!

1½ cup Raw Organic Cashew nuts soaked overnight and rinsed

1 cup fresh ripe mango, peeled and chopped

1 can organic coconut milk

3/4 cup Raw Agave Nectar

1/2 cup chopped Raw Organic Pecans

Instructions:

Night before, cover cashews with water and set aside. Rinse and chop pecans and place in dehydrator to dry overnight. Blend all ingredients <u>except pecans</u> on high speed for one 50 second cycle. Pour into 1.5 quart ice cream maker. Stir in pecans after ice cream is done. *Makes 1 quart of Butter Pecan Mango Healing Ice Cream ™.*

Healing Ice Cream™ #4
Virgin Coconut Paradise

- The Thermogenic Thyroid Enhancing Desert

3 c. distilled water
6 tablespoons extra virgin coconut oil
1 cup unsweetened organic shredded coconut
1 med ripe mango peeled and cut from seed
4 medjool dates, pitted
4 Tbls. raw agave nectar
1 tsp. non-alcoholic vanilla

Instructions:

Blend mango, water, shredded coconut and dates for two cycles until creamy. Add agave nectar, coconut oil and vanilla. Pulse for 10 seconds until blended. Pour into 1½ quart ice cream maker and freeze according to directions. *Makes 1 quart of Virgin Coconut Paradise Healing Ice Cream ™.*

Healing Ice Cream ™ #5
Acai Blueberry Purple Haze

The Anti-Aging Free Radical Fighting Desert

6 ^ 100g Sambazon Pure Acai Smoothie packets (about 3 cups)
1 pint fresh blueberries
1 c. raw agave nectar
5 fresh mint leaves

Instructions:

Blend Acai smoothie packets, blueberries, mint leaves for 1 cycle. Pour into 1½ quart ice cream maker. *Makes 1 quart of Acai Blueberry Purple Haze Healing Ice Cream ™.*

Healing Ice Cream™ #6
Maca Machoman Maple

Endocrine Enhancing Moji Amplicification Food

2½ cups distilled water
1½ cups soaked and rinsed walnuts
½ cup organic maca root powder
½ cup raw agave nectar
5 large medjool dates
1 Tbls. natural maple flavoring (non-alcoholic)

Instructions:

Soak walnuts for 4 hours to overnight, rinse and place in blender with remaining ingredients, except agave nectar and maple flavoring. Blend one cycle add agave and maple flavoring, pulse 10 seconds until blended. Pour into 1½ quart ice cream maker and freeze according to directions. *Makes 1 quart of Maca Machoman Maple Healing Ice Cream* ™.

Healing Ice Cream™ #7
Black Sesame Jing Blastoff

Power Desert for Bones, Hair and Life Essence Jing

3 c. distilled water
1 c. raw black sesame seeds, rinsed
½ c. raw pecan pieces, rinsed
4 medjool dates, pitted
½ c. raw agave nectar
¼ tsp. ground cinnamon
¼ tsp. ground cardamom
½" fresh ginger root
3 whole cloves

Instructions:

Combine all ingredients except agave nectar in blender and for two cycles until creamy. Add agave and pulse for 10 seconds to blend. Pour into 1½ quart ice cream maker and freeze according to directions. *Makes 1 quart of Black Sesame Jing Blastoff Healing Ice Cream ™.*

For: Desert "Chocolate Hazelnut Mouse"

½ c. distilled water
1 oz. RAW pealed cacao beans
½ c. raw hazelnuts
4 large pitted dates
1 tsp. non-alcoholic vanilla
½ c. pre-made Pumpkin Seed Milk

* Pour in individual dessert cups and serve warm as pudding or chill one hour before serving.

For: Desert "Chocolate Almond Mint Brew"

2c. brewed peppermint tea (cooled)
1c. soaked blanched almonds
7 RAW pealed cacao beans
4 medjool dates (pits removed)
1½ tsp. non-alcoholic vanilla
3 stems and leaves of Peppermint

For: Desert "Maca Cacao Manuka Honey Truffles"

½ c. organic maca root powder
¼. c. Manuka Honey (or another type)
½. tsp. ground cinnamon
¼ tsp. ground cardamom
1/8 tsp. ground clove powder
12 peeled organic cacao beans

Instructions:

Knead maca powder, spices and honey into stiff dough. Divide into 12 portions and roll each around a whole cacao bean. Roll in 1 Tbls. crushed cacao plus ½ tsp. maca powder to coat.

For: Desert "Creamy Sunshine Pudding"

1½ c. distilled water
1 c. raw macadamia nuts
1 orange, peeled rind only
¼ pineapple w/core & stem
½ lemon w/pith & seeds
½ fuji apple w/seeds
1 corn cut from cob
2 tsp. bee pollen

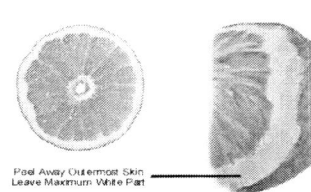

God's Super-Potent Cancer Fighting Medicine

* Pour in individual dessert cups and serve warm as pudding or chill one hour before serving.

For: Beverage "Goji Berry Milk" - Jeff's Favorite

4 oz. "Heaven Mountain" organic goji berries
2 ice cubes from distilled water
2 c. distilled water
Step 1: blend on S10 for one full cycle
Step 2: add 2 distilled water ice cubes
Step 3: blend on S10 for another full cycle

For: Beverage   "Almond Milk"

3¾ c. distilled water
¾ c. soaked raw almonds
2 tsp. agave nectar
1 ½ tsp. non-alcoholic vanilla
1/8 tsp sea salt

For: Beverage   "Hazelnut Milk"

3¾ c. distilled water
¾ c. soaked raw hazel nuts
2 tsp. agave nectar
1 ½ tsp. non-alcoholic vanilla
1/8 tsp sea salt

For: Beverage   "Oat Milk"

3¾ c. distilled water
½ c. whole oat groats
1 T. molasses
1 ½ tsp. non-alcoholic vanilla
1/8 tsp sea salt

<u>Guidelines for Nut & Grain Milks</u>: Soak the nuts and grains overnight in distilled water to release enzyme inhibitors. Place soaked nuts or grains and distilled water in blender and pulse "P" for 30 seconds. Add remaining ingredients and blend on S10 two cycles or 3 cycles. Recipes makes one quart. Refrigerate unused portion in glass container with tight fitting lid.

For: Beverage "Pumpkin Seed Milk"

3¾ c. distilled water
¾ c. raw green pumpkin seeds
2 tsp. agave nectar
1 ½ tsp. non-alcoholic vanilla
1/8 tsp sea salt

For: Beverage "Brown Rice Milk"

3¾ c. distilled water
½ c. raw short grain brown rice
2 tsp. agave nectar
1 ½ tsp. non-alcoholic vanilla
1/8 tsp. sea salt

For: Beverage "Anne's Special Golden Milk"

3¾ c. distilled water
½ c. mixed almonds, hazelnuts, walnuts
2 T. raw short grain brown rice
2 T. dried organic goji berries
½ ear of corn cut from cob
1 tsp. golden flax seed
1" slice of ginger root

For: Beverage   "Jeff's Creamy Superfood Smoothie"

1½ c. distilled water
2 Tbls. crushed cacao nibs
2 Tbls. raw pumpkin seeds
2 oz. Heaven Mountain Goji berries
½ ripe avocado - no seed
1 Tbls. organic extra virgin coconut oil
1 tsp. maca root powder
1 tsp. raw black sesame seeds
1 tsp. agave nectar (optional)
Pinch ground cinnamon

For: Beverage   "High Vibes Chocolate Milk"

2 c. distilled water
2 Tbls. Organic cacao nibs
¼ c. raw pumpkin seeds
¼ c. soaked blanched almonds
4 large pitted medjool dates
1 tsp. nonalcoholic vanilla (optional)

For: Beverage   "Almond Strawberry Delight"

1½ c. distilled water
¼ c. soaked blanched almonds
1 pint organic strawberries
1 tsp. agave nectar (optional)

For: Beverage   "Almond Apple Veggie Delight"

2 c. distilled water
½ c. soaked blanched almonds
1 ear fresh corn cut from cob
½ Fuji apple w/ seeds
½ avocado (no seed)
½ lemon w/ pith & seeds
½ slice fresh ginger root

For: Beverage   "Maca Pumpkin Seed Milk"

2 c. distilled water
½ c. raw pumpkin seeds
3 T. maca powder
1 tsp. non-alcoholic vanilla
2 T. agave nectar
Pinch of grated nutmeg for garnish
Pinch of ground cinnamon for garnish

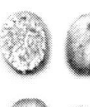

Part 5:
Soups, Salads & Bitter Mellon Dishes for Diabetics

For: Diabetes & Natural Healing "Anne's Bitter Melon Dahl"

Ingredients in Pot #1

2 c. purified water
1 c. peeled split mung beans
½ tsp. sea salt

Ingredients in Pot #2

½ c. purified water
½ tsp. turmeric powder
1 tsp. whole cumin seed
1 – 10" fresh bitter melon cubed
3 spring onions chopped w/green stalk
1/3 c. chopped cilantro
Organic extra virgin olive oil

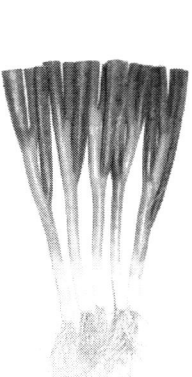

Instructions:

Rinse mung beans and place in pot with 2 c. water and ½ tsp. sea salt. Bring to boil then reduce heat and simmer 20 minutes, until almost done. While beans are cooking in large skillet over med. heat stir cumin seeds until fragrant and lightly toasted. Add ½ c. water, turmeric, cubed bitter melon and simmer for 15 minutes. Then stir in chopped spring onion and mung beans. Continue to simmer until bitter melon is tender (5-10 minutes) Add a little more water if needed. Serve warm in bowls garnished with fresh cilantro and a drizzle of olive oil. Sea Salt or Braggs to taste.

For: Diabetes & Natural Healing   "Anne's Bitter Melon Curry"

Ingredients in Pot
2 c. purified water
2 medium sized sweet potatoes
½ tsp. sea salt

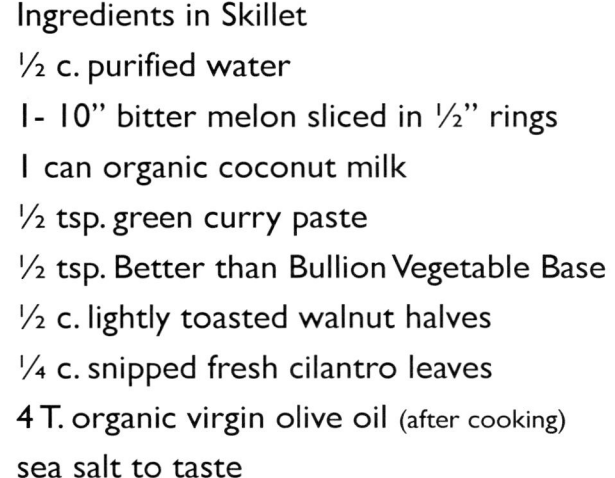

Ingredients in Skillet
½ c. purified water
1- 10" bitter melon sliced in ½" rings
1 can organic coconut milk
½ tsp. green curry paste
½ tsp. Better than Bullion Vegetable Base
½ c. lightly toasted walnut halves
¼ c. snipped fresh cilantro leaves
4 T. organic virgin olive oil (after cooking)
sea salt to taste

Instructions:

Cover sweet potatoes in water and boil until tender and easily pierced w/fork (about 30 min). When potatoes are almost done, place sliced bitter melon in single layer of large skillet with ½ c. water and over med low heat cook 15 minutes. Add coconut milk and curry paste and continue cooking 5 more minutes until bitter melon is tender. Add 2 T. of fresh cilantro and remove from heat. Slice hot sweet potatoes in half and place on two dinner plates, mash lightly and sprinkle with olive oil and sea salt. Arrange half of bitter melon rounds on top of potatoes on each plate topping each slice with a toasted walnut half. Divide coconut curry liquid and spoon over each plate. Sprinkle remaining cilantro over veggie curry and serve immediately.

For: Diabetes & Natural Healing   "Swiss Chard Salad"

6 large Swiss chard leaves
½ organic cucumber with skin
2 stalks celery
2 T. grated red beet

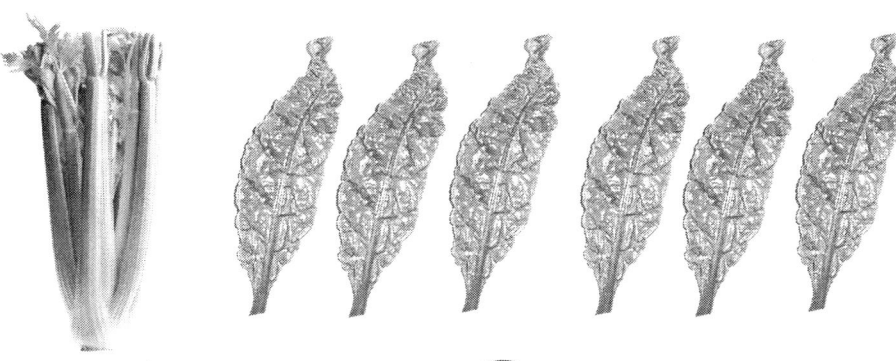

In large bowl tear leaves of Swiss chard into bite size pieces. <u>Reserve bottom 3" of chard stems for dressing</u> finely chop remaining stems to add to salad. Chop cucumber and celery add with grated beets to salad.

Live Ginger Dressing

¼ c. Purified water
½ orange bell pepper w/ seeds
3" stems cut off bottom 6 chard leaves
1" fresh ginger root
1 clove garlic
¼ tsp. sea salt
1/3 c. organic virgin olive oil

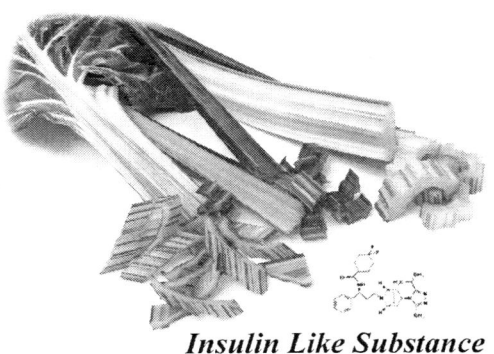

Insulin Like Substance

Instructions:

Puree all ingredients (except oil) in blender until smooth. Pour in cruet or glass jar with olive oil. Shake to blend. Refrigerate any unused portion and use within 5 days.

For: Diabetes & Natural Healing   "Watercress Salad"

3 cups snipped fresh water cress
½ organic cucumber with skin
2 T. grated red beet
2 T. grated carrot
1 small ear fresh corn cut from cob

Place all ingredients in large salad bowl.
Toss with Live Ginger Salad Dressing
or Walnut Avocado Herb Salad Dressing.

Walnut Avocado Herb Dressing

1 c. distilled water
¼ c. raw walnuts
½ small avocado
1 spring onion
1 clove garlic
½" slice fresh ginger root
2 nodes fresh cilantro
3 fresh basil leaves
2 fresh mint leaves
Pinch cayenne pepper
¼ lime w/pith

Instructions:

Puree all dressing ingredients in blender. Unused portion needs to be used within 4 hrs.

Darla's Chakra Salad
With Affirmations of Empowerment

1 stalk Romaine lettuce
1 cup blueberries
1 cup shredded carrots
1 avocado cut in chucks
½ cup sunflower seeds
2 medium tomatoes
1 cup sliced zucchini squash
1 handful sunflower sprouts
¼ cup chopped cilantro
1 cup shredded purple cabbage
¼ cup shredded beets
drizzle raw organic olive oil

Hold hands over salad and repeat:

As I eat this salad it restores and strengthens all my chakras so I can be strong to love myself and others.
I am rooted
I am full of vitality
I am powerful
I am loving
I surrender
I see things clearly
I am connected to the divine source

For: Warming Soup "Autumn Stew"

1 quart organic veggie broth
4 stalks celery chopped
6 spring onions chopped
1 butternut squash, peeled & cubed
½ bunch dinosaur kale
2 T. ghee
1 Tbls. ground cumin
1 tsp. garam marsala
½ tsp. turmeric
½ tsp. coriander
¼ tsp. cardamom
¼ tsp. cinnamon
1/8 tsp. cayenne pepper
¼ c. organic virgin olive oil
Sea salt to taste

Instructions:

In a 2 quart soup pot sauté celery and onion in ghee over med heat until onion becomes transparent (about 5 minutes). Stir in butternut squash and kale until heated through. Add broth and spices simmer 30 minutes until veggies and kale are tender. Turn off heat, mash soup slightly to thicken and add olive oil and sea salt to taste.

For: Alkalizing Soup "Creamy Cucumber Avocado Soup"

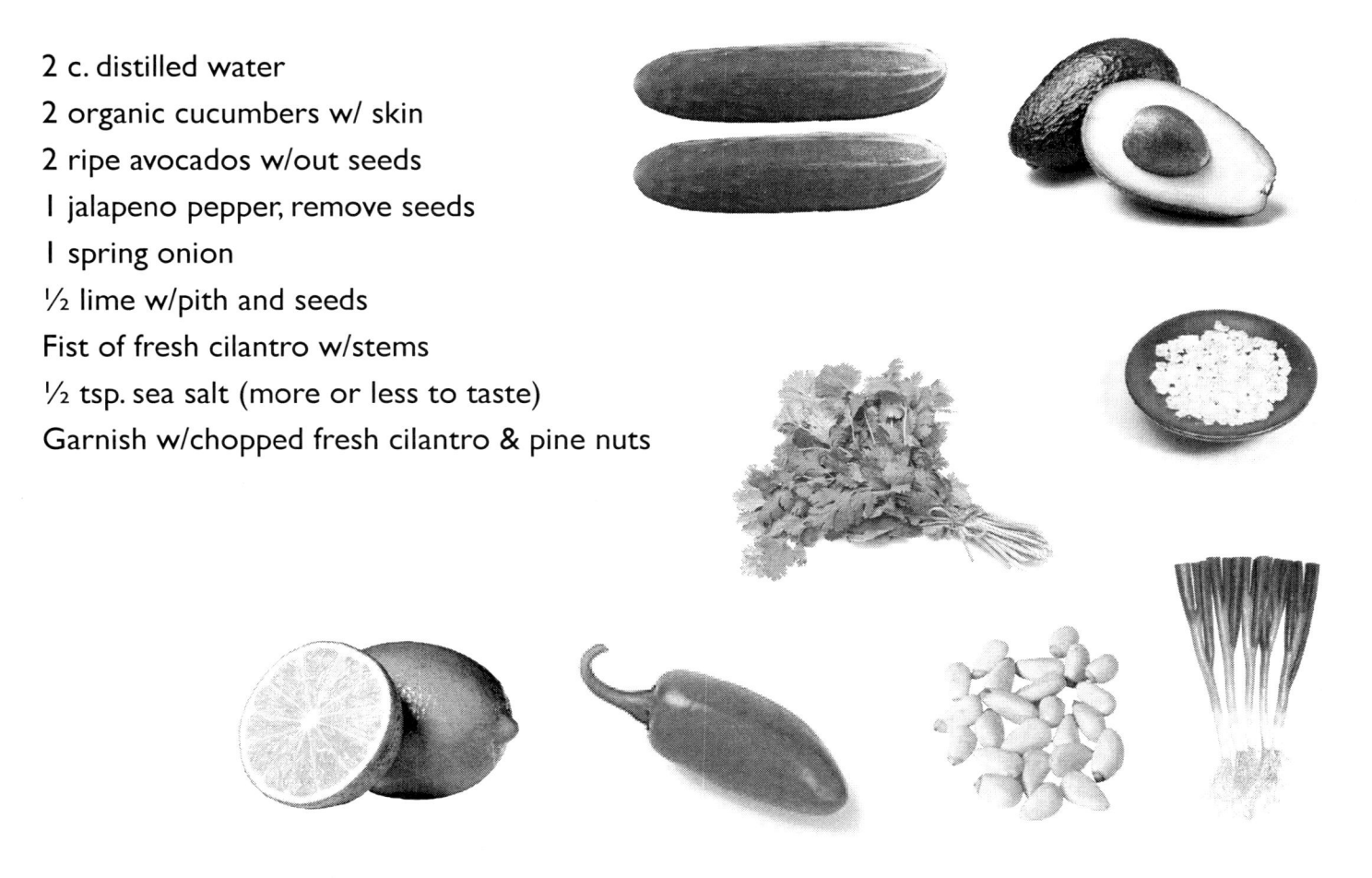

2 c. distilled water
2 organic cucumbers w/ skin
2 ripe avocados w/out seeds
1 jalapeno pepper, remove seeds
1 spring onion
½ lime w/pith and seeds
Fist of fresh cilantro w/stems
½ tsp. sea salt (more or less to taste)
Garnish w/chopped fresh cilantro & pine nuts

Instructions:

Blend 1 cycle on high speed. This soup is best served cold or room temperature. If you desire the soup to be warm simply blend another cycle and that will make it warmer.

For: Alkalizing Soup   "Creamy Asparagus Soup"

2 c. distilled water
2 c. chopped asparagus tops & tender stems
1 med. carrot
1 stalk celery
1 spring onion
3 Tbls. raw pine nuts
½ tsp. sea salt (more or less to taste)
1 tsp. fresh dill (optional)

Instructions:

Blend 1 cycle on high speed. This soup can be served cold or room temperature. If you desire the soup to be warm simply blend another cycle and that will make it warmer.

For: Alkalizing Soup   "Dietrie's Very Veggie Soup"

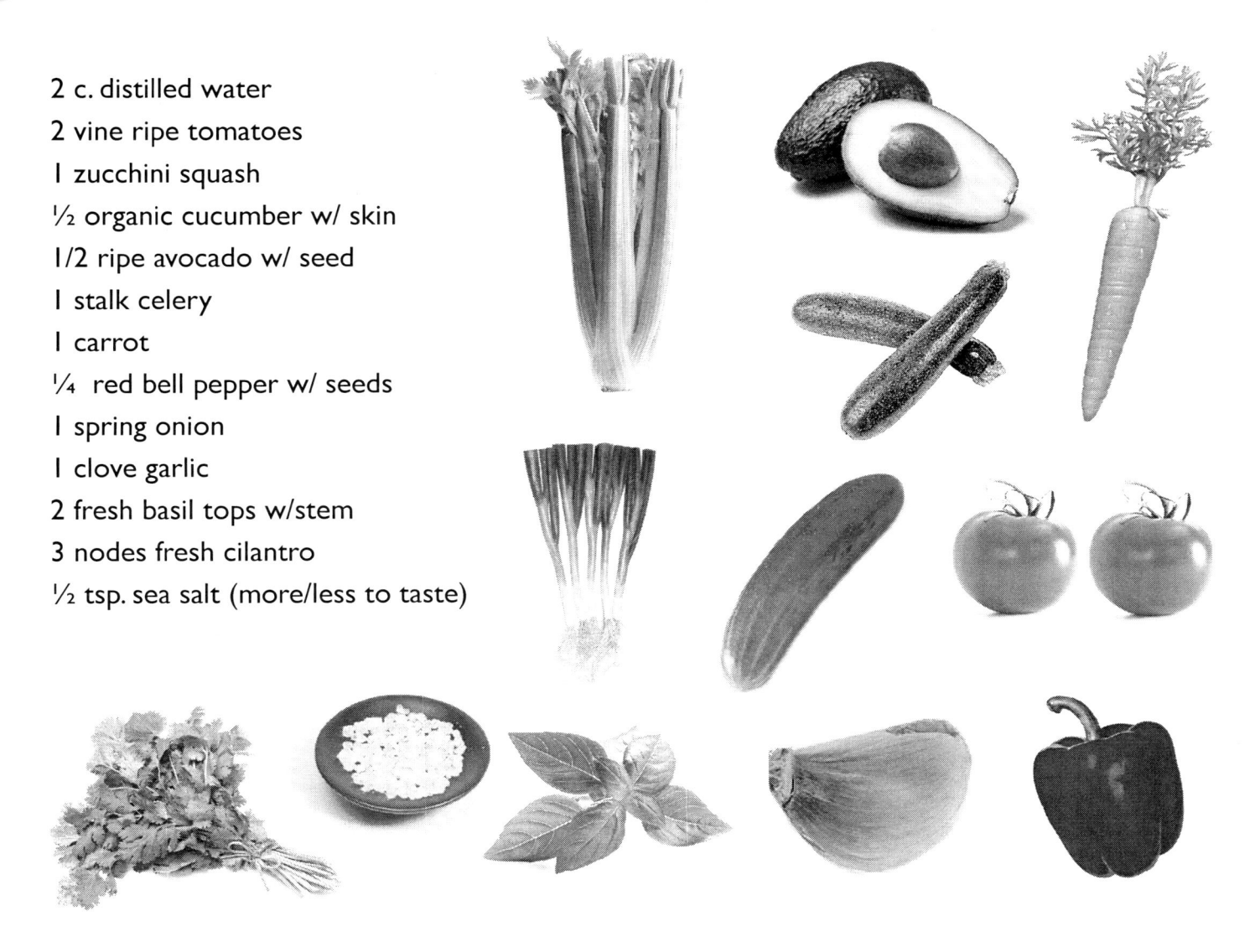

2 c. distilled water
2 vine ripe tomatoes
1 zucchini squash
½ organic cucumber w/ skin
1/2 ripe avocado w/ seed
1 stalk celery
1 carrot
¼ red bell pepper w/ seeds
1 spring onion
1 clove garlic
2 fresh basil tops w/stem
3 nodes fresh cilantro
½ tsp. sea salt (more/less to taste)

Instructions:

Blend 1 cycle on high speed. This soup can be served cold or room temperature. If you desire the soup to be warm simply blend another cycle and that will make it warmer.

For: Alkalizing Soup   "Lively Tomato Basil Soup"

1 c. distilled water
5 - 6 large vine ripe tomatoes
1 avocado without seed
2 fresh basil tops w/ stem
1 clove garlic
1 spring onion
¼ lime or lemon
2 Tbls. raw walnuts
½ tsp. sea salt (more/less to taste)

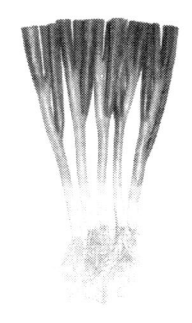

Instructions:

Blend 1 cycle on high speed. This soup can be served cold or room temperature. If you desire the soup to be warm simply blend another cycle and that will make it warmer.

For: Alkalizing Soup "Curried Cauliflower Soup"

2 c. distilled water
3 c. cauliflower
1 carrot
1 stalk celery
1 avocado w/out seed
¼ c. pumpkin seeds
1 clove garlic
½ tsp. curry powder
¼ tsp. cumin seed
Pinch cayenne pepper
½ tsp. sea salt (more or less to taste)

Instructions:

Blend 1 cycle on high speed. This soup can be served cold or room temperature. If you desire the soup to be warm simply blend another cycle and that will make it warmer.